Manifesting

Discover The Methods For Unleashing Your Boundless Capabilities,
Materializing Your Ideal Existence, And Attaining Any Aspiration You
Envision Through Effectively Channeling The Profound Influence
Bestowed By The Law Of Attraction

Albrecht Maurer

TABLE OF CONTENT

Manipulating And Regulating The Subconscious Mind

The outcome of your life is determined by the functioning of your subconscious mind. However, one has the ability to exert influence over their subconscious mind in order to actualize their aspirations and wishes. One can address and dispel preceding negative thoughts by substituting them with affirmative thoughts. Negative perceptions and beliefs can be eradicated by substituting them with a positive perception and belief framework.

Listed below are the procedural guidelines for reshaping your subconscious mind:

Acknowledge that your subconscious mind possesses the capability to bring forth the utmost desires of your heart.

1

Recognizing this fundamental truth constitutes the initial stride towards realizing your aspirations, ambitions, and yearnings. It is imperative that you embrace the notion of your ability to thoroughly transform and modify the course of your life. It is imperative that you exercise the faculty of making a decision to assume accountability for your thoughts and actions. One must possess unwavering resolve to manage and mold the subconscious mind effectively. After having made this decision, the enjoyment commences. You may commence undertaking additional measures to materialize your aspirations. You would be pleasantly astonished by the impact. You would be astounded by the expeditiousness with which you can actualize your aspirations and ideal existence.

Evaluate Your Set of Beliefs and Analyze Your Subconscious Mind

In order to exert dominion over and mold your subconscious mind, it is imperative that you devote ample time towards introspection of your present circumstances. Are you currently living the life that aligns with your greatest aspirations? Do you possess the automobile that you desire? Do you possess employment that aligns with your true passion? Is your current residence the embodiment of your ideal living space? Or do you have the job that you hate and do you have bad relationships? If you are not experiencing the desired outcomes, it is imperative to engage in introspection and thoroughly analyze your subconscious mind and thought processes, exercising utmost honesty. What latent thoughts residing in your subconscious contributed to the production of unfavorable outcomes?

"In order to evaluate your thoughts, it is necessary for you to respond to the following inquiries with utmost honesty:

Do you excessively concern yourself?

Do you tend to prioritize negative aspects and issues instead of directing your energy towards acknowledging blessings and cultivating gratitude?

Do you experience feelings of anxiety on a frequent basis?

Do you possess excessive pride, resulting in your inclination to diminish and denigrate others?

Are you motivated to pursue retribution against those who have inflicted harm and injustice upon you?

Are you experiencing feelings of anger or melancholy?

Do you experience frequent feelings of sadness?

Do you dedicate a significant amount of time pondering over your past errors?
Do you possess minimal confidence and self-regard?
Do you harbor any self-imposed limitations?

It is necessary for you to inquire and respond to a significant number of inquiries in order to ascertain the prevailing condition of your subconscious mind. The reshaping of one's subconscious mind can only be accomplished through a thorough understanding of one's present condition.

Engaging in introspection and reassessing one's past thoughts and beliefs is an additional means of assuming accountability for the information one consumes. Evaluating your thoughts and actions is akin to taking an introspective assessment of your cognitive and behavioral repertoire, in order to discern and eliminate those elements that are detrimental, superfluous, or divergent from your goals.

Revise your conduct and your system of beliefs.

If you have been unable to manifest the desires closest to your heart, it is probable that you possess limiting beliefs which give rise to self-defeating conduct. The renowned Henry Ford famously expressed, "Your belief in your own abilities, whether positive or negative, ultimately determines your outcome." Your convictions serve as the fundamental framework shaping both your present experience and the trajectory of your future. As previously explicated, these phenomena are deemed self-fulfilling prophecies due to their capacity to exert influence over one's decisions and behaviors.

Numerous individuals, devoid of aptitude, physical appearance, or cognitive prowess, are able to achieve success solely on the basis of their self-belief. In contrast, a significant number of individuals endowed with physical attractiveness, exceptional abilities, and outstanding intellect have experienced failures attributed to their constraining beliefs and diminished levels of self-assurance and self-confidence. Inhibitory beliefs impede your ability to attain the highest level of personal achievement. The following are the self-limiting beliefs that may exert adverse ramifications on your life, specifically with regard to your future:

I am not worthy

I lack the necessary aptitude and intellectual prowess to achieve success.

I am too poor

I have concerns regarding potential risks.

I am apprehensive about experiencing disappointment.

I have concerns regarding the possibility of experiencing failure.

I am suitable for this demanding position, thus I must remain committed to it.

It proves to be challenging to materialize one's aspirations.

I have no power

I can't do that

I do not possess the requisite skill or ability.

Acquiring wealth is a challenging endeavor.

I lack the necessary attributes and capabilities to realize my aspirations and ambitions.

My aspirations are ambitious and my objectives are lofty.

In order to achieve success, it is often perceived as advantageous to be born into a privileged socio-economic background.

I cannot change

I am overweight, and regrettably, I have been unable to successfully address this issue despite my efforts.

I am unable to modify my behaviors in a positive manner.

I am unable to consume nutritious food, engage in physical activity, or monitor my calorie consumption.

I am unwilling to venture into unfamiliar territory due to overwhelming fear.

This is a space where I feel comfortable and at ease.

I apologize, but I am currently quite preoccupied to attend to these matters.

The aforementioned examples represent only a limited selection. People often harbor a plethora of self-limiting and self-defeating beliefs that they repeatedly affirm to themselves on a daily basis.

Upon acknowledging these constraining beliefs, it is imperative to supplant pessimistic beliefs with optimistic ones. It is imperative that you maintain a belief in your ability to succeed. It is imperative to allocate time for the cultivation of self-esteem and confidence, as such endeavors possess extraordinary potency in materializing one's desires.

You may already possess knowledge of visualization and may have acquainted yourself with the content presented in "The Secret" through reading or viewing. Frequently, you contemplate the reasons for its lack of functionality. Here's how. Having confidence or trust in the realization of your dream or desire is sufficient. Your belief system or the depths of your subconsciousness must uphold and reinforce that unwavering faith and profound longing.

As an illustration, let us consider the case of a young lady named Kate, who harbored an enduring aspiration for the acquisition of a truly remarkable residence. Without fail, she dedicated considerable time each day to envisioning, in vivid detail, the realization of her dreams of owning an exquisite dream house. Nevertheless, despite the passage of time, she remained unable to materialize her envisioned abode. The rationale behind this is that she did not implement any measures. She failed to allocate funds towards the purchase of the property or engage in any discussions with professionals in the field of architecture. She refrained from taking action due to an internal belief of unworthiness lodged within her subconscious, despite possessing a strong desire. This belief manifests in her conviction that she lacks the capability or resources, both financial and otherwise, necessary to pursue the endeavor. As a consequence of this conviction, she refrained from taking proactive measures and failed to capitalize on the opportunities that were presented to her. As previously addressed, one's beliefs exert a significant impact on their conduct and sentiments. Although your desire may be fervent, the presence of self-defeating beliefs could pose significant challenges to the realization of your goals.

Low self-esteem and fear are the primary factors contributing to self-defeating beliefs. It is imperative to overcome any apprehension or dread surrounding the possibility of failing. Certain individuals encounter failure prior to even commencing their endeavors due to the pernicious presence of self-imposed beliefs that impose serious constraints on their potential. Facebook Inc. Furthermore, various organizations have displayed this thought-provoking inquiry prominently within their premises, encouraging their workforce to contemplate: "How would you act if fear did not hinder you?"

The key to accomplishing your dreams lies in the power of your mindset. You should cultivate an inherent sense of belief in your ability to accomplish the task. It is imperative that you maintain unwavering faith in your abilities and firmly believe that all the necessary resources are at your disposal to turn your dream into reality.

One prevalent thought pattern that frequently constrains individuals is the belief that they lack the necessary knowledge or skills to accomplish a given task. Research demonstrates that individuals who possess a positive mindset have the capacity to acquire proficiency in nearly any endeavor through self-instruction. One does not necessarily require exceptional intelligence in order to acquire proficiency in writing code, learning a different programming language, or mastering a novel skill. A positive perspective, mentality, and set of convictions are the only essentials required. Developing a computer program or acquiring proficiency in a new language can generate feelings of intimidation. Nonetheless, once you make the decision to engage in these endeavors and foster within yourself the belief that you possess the capability to succeed, the process becomes more manageable. Consider the example of Joshua Waitzkin, a former adolescent prodigy in the realm of chess. Subsequently, he discovered that our cognitive orientation and ideological framework influence the process of acquiring knowledge. If one holds the conviction in their abilities, they will manifest increased resolve and be poised to surpass expectations in virtually any endeavor. In due course, he attained the esteemed title of a Tai Chi champion and subsequently achieved mastery in Brazilian Jiu-jitsu.

You can perceive that our aspirations and longings remain unfulfilled due to the constraints imposed by our constraining convictions. As a result, it is imperative to substitute these restrictive convictions with affirmative ones. It is imperative to possess a degree of belief. It is necessary to maintain faith in one's ability. It is imperative to maintain a belief in the possibility of attaining wealth or achieving success. It is imperative for you to maintain the conviction that achieving virtually anything is within your grasp. One must have a sense of self-worth. It is imperative to recognize one's worthiness, as this establishes the conditions for one to receive the cosmic offerings.

After you have swapped out constraining beliefs with enabling beliefs, you will be astounded and taken aback by the plethora of favorable circumstances that the cosmos has prepared for you. Indeed, one has the capability to attain any desired outcome by fortifying their system of beliefs.

The Spiritual Side Of Life

Every item within your immediate environment is a marvel - every motion executed by your physical being, every inhalation, every heartbeat, every instance of food assimilation - is an extraordinary phenomenon. The capacity for thought, acquisition of knowledge, and creation that you possess is truly remarkable. It is truly remarkable how our species possesses the capability to comprehend the fundamental aspects of our environment at the atomic level. The phenomenon through which we are able to create awe-inspiring artistic masterpieces and transform our dreams into reality is nothing short of miraculous. However, what could it possibly be that motivates these phenomena? To state it unequivocally, it is of utmost importance, the life force – otherwise referred to as soul, spirit, vital energy, higher power, or divine energy... Alternatively, an alternative statement can be inserted at this point.

However, possessing a sense of sanctity—defined as a deep connection to transcendental forces and energies beyond one's self—is not truly imperative for external perception. However, it would significantly facilitate matters if one possesses a sense of spirituality. This can be attributed to the fact that every manifestation on this planet is a direct result of your affiliation with limitless wisdom. Regardless, if you diligently write down your goals each morning over an extended period of time, it is highly probable that you will materialize many of them. There is no utmost sense of necessity associated with that. Therefore, it is entirely possible to manifest something without ever delving into the realm of spirituality, deep connection, or work centered around the essence of the soul. Furthermore, it is certain that there are a multitude of individuals who negate the existence of any form of profound purpose.

Nevertheless, for those individuals who have faith, it surpasses our capacity to articulate in language. We gain a profound sense of existence through introspection, or through transpersonal encounters, perhaps facilitated by techniques such as breath work, psychotherapy, or even through the powerful moments of vibrant flowing experiences in the presence of extraordinary art or music. Furthermore, during moments of reflection, we may come across fragments of connection with the ideal, in which we gain a comprehension indicating our genuine participation in a larger entity beyond our individual selves. Simultaneously, we acknowledge our involvement in this remarkable life force. (It must be remarked that this premise is flawless for the purpose of communication.)

Such encounters can give rise to a plethora of profound inquiries, encompassing core existential questions such as personal identity and purpose. It is evident that you possess a corporeal existence, wherein your spirit or essence resides. Moreover, you also possess a profound emotional and intellectual existence, which could conceivably be localized within the brain or be phenomena arising from the mind's processes. Researchers in the field are only beginning to grasp the true magnitude of the power of the human brain. Its energy is nearly limitless: in actuality, the brain represents the most valuable aspect of each individual, serving as the remarkable and extraordinary source of everything we aspire to exhibit – or at the very least, the means by which it can be made apparent. Furthermore, one can deliberately embark on a journey within oneself to enter the realm of one's soul, using practices such as introspection and introspective representation to access an alternative way of existing in the world.

It is possible that by engaging in this practice, one may come to comprehend the true essence of the saying that resonates in this manner: "We are not merely corporeal beings occasionally engaging in spiritual matters, but rather profound beings continuously experiencing physical challenges." Countless literary works throughout time have emphasized the imperative for individuals to lead a spiritual existence, or at the very least, to incorporate a spiritual dimension into their lives. The rationale behind this concept is that a profound and disciplined way of living teaches us that the divine entity, whether referred to as God, Universal Intelligence, Power Greater Than Ourselves, Cosmic Consciousness, Great Mystery, Oneness, Vital Force, or any other name, possesses an omniscient, omnipotent, and omnipresent nature that cannot be evaded. Moreover, as you are undoubtedly aware, this implies that this capability is inherently ingrained within you, encompassing your entirety, while simultaneously being a component of the restriction itself.

Clearly, the more seamlessly you are able to establish a connection with The Universal Intelligence, the more effortlessly you will be able to actualize your desired manifestations. This is because the accessibility to the level where your subconscious mind can communicate with universal energy is significantly more readily attainable to you. It is advisable to establish a regular spiritual practice, as doing so aids in the remembrance of one's true essence, which is an integral component of the interconnected universe. Marc Allen, the author of The Millionaire Course, from which these ideas are derived, elaborates on his profound routine that has evolved over time, transitioning from a simplistic morning ritual to a profound state of relaxation, heightened awareness, guided meditation, and imaginative visualization.

If you approach the endeavor with the intention of doing so, you will be able to easily find your own spiritual practice. There exist an extensive array of alternatives, rendering it challenging to provide a comprehensive selection at this moment. However, personally, I adhere to the practice of inhabiting the garden each morning to express gratitude towards the various archetypes that resonate within me - encompassing The Lover, The Magician, The Warrior, and most importantly, The Sovereign, who governs the course of my existence. Developing appreciation is equally crucial to me, as it enables me to remain cognizant of the fact that despite any personal perspectives or apprehensions I may have regarding the state or future of the world, there are numerous reasons for which I should express gratitude, outweighing any pessimistic sentiments. (As evidenced from the assessment, appreciation is widely regarded as a pivotal element for achieving a successful presentation.)

Do Not Extend Assistance To Others Without Safeguarding And Preserving Your Personal Energy.

The message expounded upon in this chapter may diverge from conventional thinking for certain individuals. However, it might also provide significant solace and alleviate their internal states.

Allow us to clarify something before delving into the matter at hand: indeed, we hold the conviction of assisting others. The authentic inclination to assist others, supported by consonant conduct and righteous motives, elevates the energy levels of all parties concerned.

However, recognizing that this message will reach a significant audience composed of compassionate individuals, we find it more fitting to delve into a more comprehensive exploration of the importance of adopting the correct mindset and heartset when providing assistance to others.

Here is our analysis of topics that we believe merit discussion and possess the potential to benefit Elena's esteemed audience members who are undertaking a similar transformative voyage:

-When are you in a position to help others? Is it advisable to sacrifice your personal needs in order to assist others?

- Is it ethically justifiable to offer assistance to others for financial gain?

-Is it solely one's sense of obligation that should compel them to assist others?

- "Methods for safeguarding oneself against the manipulative influences exerted by individuals?"

-How can one ensure that their actions are aligned with the correct course of action, providing assistance to someone in a manner that is advantageous to them?

- Is it possible to provide assistance to someone without taking any action?

- Is it possible for you to offer assistance to someone simply through your presence?

- Is it socially acceptable to proudly discuss one's assistance to others and the extent of their impact on a formal level?

-Is it appropriate to assist others solely for the purpose of doing so?

First and foremost, let us commence with the most crucial matter at hand...

- At what point are you able to provide assistance to others? Do you believe it is appropriate to forgo personal needs in order to assist others?

The concise response is that you should prioritize assisting yourself in the first place. It is just as straightforward as that. Although some may express dissent and claim that it lacks spiritual significance, we posit the following viewpoint: in order to genuinely assist others, it is imperative to possess the ability to do so.

Hence, it is imperative that you prioritize your own well-being. In order to contribute towards philanthropic causes by financially supporting preferred charitable organizations, it is essential to possess an ample amount of resources that adequately cater to both personal and communal needs. Even if one does not possess materialistic inclinations, it remains imperative to amass sufficient financial resources to procure sustenance and secure suitable accommodation, would you not agree?

In order to make a meaningful impact on a larger community, by utilizing financial resources as a means, it is imperative to prioritize one's own financial stability as well as the financial stability of any organization or philanthropic endeavor one intends to establish or endorse.

Certainly, currency serves as merely one instrument at your disposal to offer assistance to others. It possesses immense potency and can swiftly cater to individuals necessitating provisions such as sustenance, refuge, or medical attention. There is no room for uncertainty regarding that matter. It also possesses the capability to contribute towards one's educational expenses, thereby assisting individuals in attaining an improved economic outlook for themselves and their respective families.

Our primary objective is to illuminate the multitude of means available to assist individuals in need. There exist a multitude of methods through which one can assist oneself and others.

The key lies in selecting the vehicle that provides a sense of alignment with your preferences and disposition.

As an illustration, certain individuals prefer dedicating their time to aiding others through engaging in voluntary work for a charitable cause or any other organization they endorse. Certain individuals have a propensity for providing monetary assistance or nourishment to those without a permanent place of residence. While individuals might have limited financial means, they can still contribute valuable emotional and psychological assistance, aiding those in need to alter their mindset and foster a sense of optimism.

Numerous individuals will argue that in order to assist others on a larger magnitude, an ample amount of financial resources is the sole prerequisite. Furthermore, as previously stated, aiding individuals at a fundamental level and facilitating enhancement of their living conditions can be expeditiously achieved through financial support.

However, while it may sound critical, it should be acknowledged that in certain cases, individuals may receive financial assistance and make temporary improvements to their circumstances, only to ultimately revert back to their previous state of financial instability.

Why? Due to the fact that they have not altered their habits, mindsets, and energetic principles by which they conduct themselves. They have not altered their level of consciousness.

Therefore, it is of utmost significance to provide spiritual and mental support to others by aiding them in the process of elevating their consciousness. This is precisely what we believe is imperative for the betterment of the world. By engaging with literature centered around the concepts of the Law of Attraction, mindset, spirituality, and self-development, you align yourself with a select group of individuals exhibiting a heightened state of consciousness.

Naturally, it is not suggested that one should develop a sense of superiority as a result, nor should individuals pass judgment upon those who do not engage in similar reading materials.

However, upon further contemplation, it becomes evident that you possess the capacity to elevate the vibrational frequency of our planet. You possess all the necessary knowledge to enact a personal transformation, actualize your aspirations, optimize your personal growth, and contribute to the betterment of others through the dissemination of your expertise.

It's really up to you how you decide to approach it. Certain individuals enjoy facilitating workshops for their local community. Certain individuals derive pleasure from disseminating their expertise through various mediums such as literature, videos, or digital platforms. The advancements in technology are revolutionizing societies and have the potential to greatly assist individuals, even in their moments of rest. For instance, you have the option to create a video elucidating a spirituality subject that you have been acquiring knowledge on, or alternatively, you could produce a video that inspires or motivates individuals, and subsequently distribute it to a global audience.

Subsequently, the content forged by your efforts has the capability to disseminate your message and continue to motivate others, even during times when you are occupied with other engagements.

This exemplifies the marvel (and influence) of technology!

Furthermore, imparting your knowledge and distinctive narrative has the potential to instill hope, bring about profound changes, or even usher in a complete transformation in the lives of others. Subsequently, they undergo self-improvement and subsequently exhibit enhanced regard towards both themselves and others. Their metamorphosis yields a cumulative impact.

This possesses significant potency and has the capacity to overhaul consciousness and enhance the overall vibrational state of the collective.

Conclusion? There is no definitive answer or incorrect approach. If you feel compelled, there exist numerous avenues through which you can offer assistance to others. It is essential to identify a method that resonates with your personal convictions and preferences. Each individual possesses a unique set of skills or talents that can contribute to the greater good of society.

Regardless of the medium you select, please prioritize self-help. If you find yourself unable to provide assistance to others, direct the entirety of your attention, or at least the majority of it, towards aiding yourself.

- Is it ethically justifiable to offer assistance to others as a commercial endeavor and levy fees for it?

Indeed, without a doubt, it is undoubtedly so.

If you possess the aspiration to become a humane-oriented entrepreneur and establish a company or enterprise that aids others, do not hesitate to pursue it. Disentangle yourself from any sense of shame or guilt associated with monetizing your services.

Is your hairdresser burdened by a sense of guilt when billing you for their services rendered on your hair? What is your arrangement with your handyman, mechanic, or any other service provider that you engage?

However, there remains a considerable amount of criticism regarding the practice of requesting payment for spiritual services or endeavors stemming from deep-seated emotions and beliefs.

Certainly, we are not dictating your course of action. Our primary objective is to stimulate your intellectual and emotional receptivity in order to facilitate the acquisition of the answers you seek. It entails prioritizing one's intuition and acting in accordance with one's personal values.

We have previously discussed the topics of finances and prosperity in the preceding chapter. We touched upon the concept that money, by its intrinsic nature, is impartial. However, when placed in the custody of virtuous individuals who prioritize compassion and empathy, it possesses the potential to exclusively yield positive outcomes in our society.

In concurrence with this notion, consider the potential transformation our world may undergo, alongside the multitude of positive outcomes that could arise from an increased prevalence of businesses driven by compassion and empathy. Organizations that engage in ethical practices provide competitive remuneration to their workforce and deliver exceptional products and services that positively impact individuals' lives. Those businesses have the capacity to create positive impact and foster satisfaction among all stakeholders.

Therefore, if it resonates deep within you and aligns with your purpose, grant yourself the authorization to commence by relinquishing any remorse associated with setting prices for your products or services.

Ultimately, it hinges on introspection regarding one's authentic desires and overcoming any obstacles pertaining to those desires through proactive and congruent steps. It is important to bear in mind that one should not be subjected to judgement, as it is both imperative and secure to embrace one's authentic self and pursue one's own aspirations.

However, as is customary, the pivotal factor lies in the choices made and prioritizing one's personal welfare. Do you recall the remarks made at the commencement of this chapter? One cannot assist others without first attending to one's own needs. Simultaneously, it does not revolve around adhering to prevalent fads. As we disseminate this communication, we acknowledge the pervasive impact of social media on individuals who are increasingly susceptible to external influences. Numerous individuals opt to venture into entrepreneurship or establish coaching enterprises based on the perception that it is an obligation or societal expectation. But they are not passionate about what they do.

Kindly prioritize the cultivation of your inner thoughts and emotions. It has been reiterated on numerous occasions that aiding others should evoke a sense of fulfillment, and there exists an infinite array of avenues to accomplish this. Therefore, in the event that you find yourself trapped in a professional endeavor that fails to ignite your passion or yield satisfactory results, and you are contemplating pursuing a different path, empower yourself to grant permission for such a change. Choose yourself first. Aiding others need not involve self-sacrifice or enduring hardship. It ought to manifest as an authentic reflection of your essence.

Furthermore, it is not necessary to focus on engaging in exceptional endeavors. If that is not your vocation, it is not necessary to focus on achieving celebrity status as an entrepreneur or renowned coach.

Extraordinary accomplishments can be achieved through the performance of everyday tasks or occupations. There exist numerous individuals of ordinary standing who remain undisclosed, devoid of fame and the scrutiny of camera lenses capturing their altruistic actions; nevertheless, they actively engage in numerous benevolent acts. Why? Due to their diligent commitment and enthusiastic dedication, they consistently endeavor to tackle any job or task with a positive and vibrant approach.

The conclusion? You have the capability to provide assistance to others in any task, occupation, or enterprise that you undertake. When undertaking any task, it is essential to consider the recipients involved and the ways in which your efforts will contribute to their well-being.

It revolves around the energy you exude. You have the potential to assume the role of a healthcare professional, mentor, financial expert, emergency responder, philanthropist, culinary expert, restaurant server, custodial staff, chief executive officer, or educator. Ensure that whatever task you undertake, you approach it with diligence and focus. Bless everyone around you. One may utilize their customary occupation or engage in various activities, including personal interests such as hobbies, as means to disseminate optimistic energy and provide assistance to others.

Some individuals find comfort and a sense of stability in maintaining regular employment that adequately fulfills their financial requirements. By doing so, they can allocate their free time toward the pursuit of personal aspirations or engaging in altruistic endeavors. However, there are individuals who opt to devote their entire time and energy towards establishing a business that not only sustains their livelihood, but also provides support for their employees and families, while simultaneously offering impactful products or services.

Continuously assess what aligns with your needs and circumstances. It is crucial to bear in mind that one has the ability to bring forth anything they desire, provided that their objective genuinely originates from within, rather than being influenced by others.

Elena consistently suggests allocating time for serene introspection and contemplation, in order to connect with your genuine aspirations and identify the individual path to attain them. There is no definitive answer or moral judgment.

Do not succumb to the pressure of relinquishing your current employment due to the influence of certain virtual mentors who proclaim it as the sole pathway to attaining prosperity, achievement, and contentment. However, concurrently, if you are truly destined to establish your own enterprise, do not harbor feelings of guilt when it comes to pricing your services and fully committing to your area of expertise.

Different individuals have varying preferences and inclinations. Take ownership of your actions and embrace your true identity.

The primary focus of this literary work lies in the inexhaustible capacity for empowerment. There are countless methods through which one can lead their life with the intention of fulfilling their life's purpose and aiding others, simply by embracing their true selves and exerting their utmost efforts in their endeavors, while operating at their optimal vibration.

- Is lending assistance to others solely a matter of obligation?

A small minority of individuals possess an awareness of this fundamental spiritual principle. The greater the exertion of effort towards tasks that are undesired, the greater the likelihood of generating unfavorable consequences.

Naturally, it is not our intention to elicit feelings of guilt regarding your previous choices. And we genuinely comprehend that individuals consistently strive to achieve the utmost with the resources at their disposal. Simultaneously, the influence of societal expectations and conformity to stereotypical norms can lead us astray from our intended path.

The foremost principle to bear in mind is to provide assistance to others should you wish to do so. However, it is essential to prioritize attending to your personal needs beforehand. Additionally, assisting others should not be approached as a contest or a competitive endeavor. It does not need to revolve around self-sacrifice.

- "Methods for safeguarding oneself against the manipulative energies emitted by others."

The initial step that is required of you is to consistently evaluate and examine your thoughts and emotions. Put simply, one must possess a profound command over their perceptiveness. Your consciousness shall liberate you.

There exist varying degrees of consciousness, and ensuring that you function from the most elevated level will guide you towards the appropriate path, irrespective of your endeavors or location.

Regardless of the means of transportation you select to offer assistance to others, it is crucial to remain mindful of the following principle: if your genuine purpose is to aid someone, ensure that your actions are aimed at empowering them to be self-sufficient. That represents the utmost level of assistance that you can provide, regardless of your efforts. Furthermore, your assistance enables individuals to develop and achieve autonomy.

Make a concerted effort to operate from this heightened state of awareness to experience profound transformations in your reality.

- "How can one ensure their actions are ethical and effective in aiding individuals who stand to gain from their assistance?"

So, first things first. How can one determine if one is engaged in morally correct actions? It is essential to have self-awareness regarding one's principles, values, and personal convictions. It is imperative to formulate and adhere to a personal life philosophy. It is essential for one to exemplify their beliefs.

When one possesses self-awareness and remains anchored in their authenticity, they naturally draw individuals who possess self-identity and clarity about their desires.

And you are able to draw in individuals who possess a genuine admiration for your efforts and assistance.

- Are you capable of providing assistance without engaging in any novel or exceptional actions?

Indeed, that is a viable option as well. Ultimately, it is not the actions themselves that hold significance, but rather the manner in which they are carried out. One can provide assistance to others simply by displaying one's authentic self.

Inspiring and motivating others can be seen as a way of providing assistance or support. You have the ability to serve as a source of inspiration and motivation merely through your authentic self. You have the opportunity to embrace and embody your authentic truth while diligently pursuing your rightful vocation to the best of your abilities.

If you are not currently aware of your vocation, please refrain from concerning yourself with it at this time. Merely establish a purposeful aim to locate it. At present, grant yourself the indulgence of conscientiously delving into diverse possibilities, acquiring fresh knowledge, and engaging in spiritual pursuits through the execution of mundane duties or the pursuit of an ordinary occupation with extraordinary dedication.

A Comprehensive Sequential Tutorial On Crafting Abundance Checks With Consistent Efficacy

It is an exceedingly straightforward procedure.

There exist two approaches to writing manifestation checks, and we shall elaborate upon each approach to enable you to select the method that most aligns with your preferences.

Approach 1: The Conventional Approach

This is the conventional approach that has been transmitted through successive generations.

This methodology was employed during a time when banks or checkbooks were non-existent.

Simply obtain a sheet of paper or a check, and proceed to inscribe your name, the desired amount, the specified date for disbursement, and the rationale behind your request.

Nevertheless, the primary distinction between this approach and the subsequent approach that I shall demonstrate pertains to the requirement of composing it within the initial 24 hours subsequent to the onset of the new lunar phase.

The lunar cycle encompasses a duration of approximately 29.53 days, during which the moon undergoes eight distinct phases. These stages delineate the lunar location at any given moment during its orbital pathway.

As the moon progresses in its celestial trajectory, the lunar phases undergo alteration.

It commences with the phase of the new moon.

New Moon: This phase denotes the commencement of the moon's orbital journey around the earth. The lunar surface is currently only partially discernible from the vantage point of our planet.

Waxing Crescent: During this phase, the moon initiates its progression towards reaching a state of fullness.

Currently, a minute portion of the lunar surface is radiating light, granting us the ability to behold approximately one-third of the moon's entirety from our vantage point on Earth.

First Quarter: At this juncture, the moon has traversed one-quarter of its orbit around the earth.

Approximately 50 percent of the moon is currently visible from the vantage point of Earth, a phenomenon commonly referred to as the phase of half-moon.

Waxing Gibbous: During the waxing phase, the moon increases in size as it approaches complete fullness. The term 'gibbous' denotes a form that is of a lesser dimension than a complete circle yet surpasses that of a semi-circle.

Full Moon: During the phase of the full moon, the lunar orbit has reached its conclusion, resulting in the entire moon being fully illuminated and observable without the aid of any optical instruments.

The moon assumes a sizable circular shape, and conventionally, this signifies the conclusion of a lunar cycle.

Waning Gibbous: The waning gibbous phase denotes the gradual diminishment of the moon's size as it proceeds in the counterclockwise direction, retracing its path towards the new moon stage.

Third Quarter: The third quarter corresponds to the lunar phase that is diametrically opposed to the half-moon phase. Half of the moon is visible from the vantage point of the Earth, though it appears in a diametrically opposed orientation.

Waning Crescent: The waning phase of the moon is characterized by its diminishing size, gradually adopting the distinctive crescent form reminiscent of a boat or a banana.

This indicates that the moon is in the process of transitioning towards the new moon phase.

Obscured Lunar Phase: The obscured lunar phase occurs when the moon undergoes a near-complete disappearance for a period of approximately 1-4 days, preceding its emergence as a new moon.

I took time to explain what the moon phases are because each phase comes with a unique energy that can be used to manifest different things.

The energy derived from the new moon is frequently harnessed to bring about the manifestation of fresh endeavors and opportunities, while the traditional purpose of the energy encompassing the full moon pertains to the expulsion of undesired elements from one's existence.

Therefore, in adherence to tradition, we make use of the occurrence of the new moon to effectively manifest our desires by means of employing our law of abundance manifestation checks.

Therefore, if one desires to employ the conventional approach, it is imperative to transcribe one's checks during the initial 24 hours subsequent to the commencement of the new lunar cycle.

You have the ability to monitor the lunar phases in order to determine the opportune moment to write your manifestation checks related to the law of abundance.

How to Generate Your Law of Abundance Checks Utilizing the Conventional Procedure

First step: Select a moment within the initial 24 hours of the lunar cycle when the moon is not visible in the sky.

It is possible to schedule it at any time of the day, whether it be morning, night, or evening- the decision is entirely up to you.

It is of utmost importance to dedicate a certain amount of time to the ritual during which you will not encounter any disruptions or distractions, ideally for a minimum duration of 30 minutes.

Proceed to physically generate your abundance checks by printing them out.

Included with the purchase of the paperback edition of this book are 100 manifestation checks, which you may utilize.

Utilize a pair of scissors to precisely extract one of the cheques, subsequently putting it to use.

If you have purchased the eBook edition, you may acquire the paperback edition from this source to avail yourself of the pre-designed manifestation checks.

Alternatively, if that is not the case, feel free to utilize any available sheet of paper or parchment paper.

Proceed to Step Three: Indicate your personal identification in the designated section labeled 'Payment'.

In the event that you are utilizing a sheet of paper, kindly inscribe the phrase 'Pay to' and proceed to inscribe your name directly preceding it.

Fourth step: Within the designated field for monetary value, inscribe a precise sum that you aspire to bring into reality.

If you desire to materialize something other than monetary wealth, kindly inscribe your intentions within the designated container.

My customary practice entails conceptualizing a monetary value commensurate with the desired outcome, which I proceed to inscribe within the designated enclosure.

For instance, when I endeavor to materialize something that does not have a quantifiable value, such as a joyful and healthy companionship, I merely inscribe "A content and thriving relationship with my ideal partner" within the designated space.

Step Five: In the designated space marked as "memo", kindly inscribe the phrase "paid in full".

This conveys a signal to the cosmos that you desire completeness and immediacy, rejecting the notion of partial fulfillment or gradual progression.

Step Six: In the designated field labeled 'signature,' please inscribe 'The Universe'.

If you are utilizing the enclosed checks, they have already been duly signed for your convenience.

Proceed to complete the sections corresponding to the dates. Please specify a "scheduled completion date" that reflects the deadline by which you desire to realize your manifestations. Nonetheless, this does not imply that your manifestations are constrained to occurring exclusively before or after the designated date.

While it is permissible to abstain from providing an answer, I am fervently in favor of presenting explicit directives to the universe. The greater the level of specificity in your instructions, the more lucid your message becomes, thus facilitating the realization of your desires.

Therefore, it is important to consistently include a date, while also exercising practicality in setting realistic timelines. It is advisable to set a date in the future, allowing ample time for the universe to manifest its workings.

Please refrain from issuing a check with today's date and avoid writing it as well. That proposition appears to lack feasibility and is unlikely to yield positive outcomes.

Step Eight: In the designated field for the check number, place the numerical sequence "000 333 444 11111" followed by your date of birth.

Therefore, in the event that your date of birth is January 1st, 1985, the designated check number assigned to you will be "000 333 444 11111 01011985".

These numbers can be referred to as angelic numbers. By incorporating these numbers into your checks, you imbue your manifestation rituals with a spiritual essence, amplifying the potency of your law of abundance manifestation checks.

Angelic entities utilize the system of angelic numerology for the purpose of establishing communication channels with individuals of the human race. Due to the universality of numbers, angels employ them as a means of establishing communication with us and imparting their presence. Given the intended communication, they would transmit designated, encoded messages utilizing a numerical sequence aligned with numerology.

Every sequence denotes distinct meanings.

000 symbolizes divinity and embodies the boundless essence of the divine.

In the realm of spiritual symbolism, the numerical sequence 333 represents the esteemed presence of ascended masters or saints, while the numerical sequence 444 signifies the celestial beings known as angels.

By inscribing these numerical values upon your check, you are effectively transmitting a covert communication to the divine entities of God, the heavenly messengers, and the revered saints, beseeching their intervention and expediting the realization of your desired outcomes.

Recording your date of birth bears a resemblance to appending your identification card to the cheque. Prior to cashing a check at a financial institution, it is customary for the customer to be requested to provide their identification card, thus allowing the cashier to verify that the check is being dispensed to the rightful recipient. When you indicate your date of birth on the check, you are affirming your identity as the legitimate recipient of the manifestation. You desire to receive your wishes directly from the universe, bypassing any intermediaries representing you.

Step Nine: Express appreciation by inscribing the words 'Thank you' on the check.

Step Ten: Proceed to compose a selection of positive affirmations on the reverse side of the check.

Herein are several instances of positive statements that can be inscribed on your monetary instrument:

I am receptive to a wealth of opportunities.

I am deserving of success and abundance.

I express gratitude for the forthcoming blessings and prosperity that are destined to enter my life."

Subsequently, the ensuing actions may be deemed optional if one does not hold a belief in their efficacy.

There are individuals who hold reservations about using crystals or candles as instruments for manifestation, and their perspective is considered acceptable.

However, adhering to traditional practices has consistently demonstrated expedited outcomes in materializing my intentions, thereby substantiating the efficacy of employing these tools.

Nevertheless, it is not suitable for all individuals. The absence of crystals or candles in your manifestation exercises will not impede their effectiveness.

The most important thing is having faith and trust in whatever method you choose. So, do you!

However, for those who, like myself, maintain a belief in utilizing candles and crystals to add an element of excitement, here is some guidance:

Eleventh Step: Employ Crystals Known for their Capacity to Draw Prosperity

Crystals like green aventurine, citrine, jade, sunshine, or tiger's eyes are very great for attracting abundance and prosperity.

Position the crystals atop the completed check, allowing for a duration of 30 minutes to one hour for the infusion of energy from the crystals to transpire.

Assume a seated position in front of the monetary instruments and precious stones. Proceed to gently close your eyes, and engage in a mental exercise wherein you vividly imagine the act of depositing and ultimately utilizing the funds from your check, thereby immersing yourself in the tangible existence of the desired outcome you are currently striving to bring into fruition.

In order to employ candles, it is necessary to make proper arrangements, including the acquisition of candles and their subsequent illumination, prior to commencing the visualization exercise.

The subsequent procedure will guide you in the preparation of your candle.

The twelfth step entails the utilization of green candles, which are specifically chosen to evoke notions of prosperity and abundance. Therefore, it is recommended to employ green candles for this purpose.

You must ensure the candle is adorned with botanical elements and fragrant essences specifically designed to invoke and attract prosperity and abundance.

Apply the oils evenly to the surface of the candle, starting at the base and working your way towards the top.

Once you have finished applying the oils, proceed to take a generous amount of the herbs and gently spread them around the candles using a consistent upward motion, following the same technique previously employed. The herbs ought to adhere to the oil.

You may proceed with igniting the candle, positioning it in proximity to the crystals, and subsequently assuming a seated position in front of it for the purpose of visualization.

One can repetitively recite affirmations while engaging in visualization.

Please perform this task for a duration of 30 minutes or until the candle is completely consumed by the flame.

Suitable herbs for utilization comprise Bergamot, Ginger, and Patchouli.

Regarding oils, viable options include Frankincense essential oil, Patchouli oil, Rose Oil, and Jasmine.

One may opt to create a fusion of oils, combining 2 drops of Patchouli, 3 drops of Frankincense, 2 drops of Clary Sage Oil, and 3 drops of Wild Orange.

Alternatively, you have the option of combining 3 drops of Wild Orange with 3 drops of Frankincense, adding 1 drop of Cinnamon, and including 2 drops of ginger.

Upon the occasion of the upcoming new moon, retrieve your abundance check and reflect upon the extent of abundance you have acquired during the preceding month. Express gratitude for all monetary contributions you receive, including anticipated earnings. Doing so will convey to the cosmos that you are prepared to accept even greater abundance of what you already possess.

Discerning The Deceptions Of The Real World

Up to this point in the chapter, we have delved into the concept of inner silence and examined the intricacies of the human mind. Additionally, we explored the notion of directing our attention towards objects that comprise the realm of human experience. We deliberated upon the notion that the phenomenal realm encompasses all that is within the realm of cognitive perception or sensory detection. The majority of individuals experience their existence primarily from a phenomenal standpoint. To put it differently, our consciousness is constrained within the realm of physical manifestation.

As our attention gravitates towards the realm of form, we have developed an inclination to align ourselves with the world of form. Our perception and understanding of our own identities are frequently shaped by the phenomenal aspects of life. Allow me to provide you with an illustration.

Joe is in the process of commuting to work, operating his vehicle, when he encounters a situation wherein he is abruptly obstructed by an inattentive driver. Joe becomes enraged and utters profanities towards the other driver. Upon Joe's arrival at his workplace, his boss notifies him that he will be receiving a bonus. Upon receiving this news, Joe is filled with joy. Subsequently, Joe receives a phone call from a challenging client. Joe becomes frustrated. Ultimately, Joe returns to his residence and is warmly received by his loved ones. Currently, Joe experiences feelings of affection and encouragement.

Throughout the course of the day, Joe encountered a myriad of emotional states, with each state eliciting a distinct sense of self in Joe. Additionally, it was his conviction that the fluctuations in his emotional well-being stemmed from the circumstances he had encountered. He ascribes these alterations to the other motorist, the incentive, the challenging client, and his family. Joe serves as a testament to the profound influence that the circumstances and occurrences in our lives have on our personal identity. As perpetual transformation is an inherent element of existence, our perception of personal identity remains in a state of flux. At times, we may experience fleeting moments of euphoria, believing ourselves to be invincible, only to be consequently overwhelmed by the tumultuous winds of change.

Now, contemplate your own existence. How has your life transformed since your early childhood? Have your thoughts changed? Have your beliefs changed? Have your relationships changed? Has your body changed? Has your perception of the world been altered? Has your self-perception undergone any alterations? Every encounter you have ever had has undergone alteration to varying degrees. The state of existence in life is characterized by perpetual change and flux, especially when it pertains to the observable and perceptible aspects.

To assert that all aspects of existence undergo transformation, although compelling, remains insufficient. What evidence do you have to support the notion that change is taking place? You are cognizant of the fact that alteration transpires in a manner resembling your familiarity with the entity featured in the preceding exercise. You possess knowledge of change as a result of your awareness. Nevertheless, in order for

70

you to possess an understanding of transformation, it is imperative that you possess an awareness of that which remains immutable. Is it possible to comprehend something without understanding its counterpart? How can one comprehend the concept of cold without having an understanding of hot? One cannot truly understand serenity without also understanding rage.

There exists within your being a facet that possesses an innate cognizance of alteration, encompassing the physical, mental, and emotional transformations that you experience. The rationale behind the consciousness of transformation within this facet of your being is its inherent immutability. Only the immutable can apprehend the mutable. In what other manner could change possibly be recognized? There exists within the depths of your being an inherent aspect that transcends all conceptions and resides in the serene realm of silence. The concept I am referring to is beyond the grasp of the human intellect, as it exists outside the realm of perception. To assert that something is non-phenomenal is tantamount to asserting its imperceptibility to the senses or incapability of being comprehended by the faculties of the mind.

The phenomenon commonly recognized as "reality" pertains to the continuous unfolding of life, a process observed by one's transcendent self. The concept of an absolute reality is absent; instead, what we perceive as reality is an ever-evolving manifestation of consciousness. The fallacious nature of our perception lies in the fact that we inhabit a corporeal realm in which we exist as distinct individuals. We perceive ourselves as distinct entities, set apart from fellow individuals, inanimate entities, and the surroundings. Due to our inherent sense of individuality, we strive to attain the material possessions present in the physical world under the premise that they hold the key to our happiness and liberation from emotional distress.

Given the impermanence of all phenomena, the human experience encompasses a feeling of loss or disillusionment in the face of change. We are akin to a hamster trapped on a perpetual wheel. Regardless of our speed or effort, we are unable to attain that elusive destination where enduring tranquility resides. We have succumbed to the misperceptions of reality, wherein we delude ourselves with the belief that external entities possess the ability to fulfill our desired experiences.

Attaining true serenity is rooted in anchoring ourselves in the steadfast, while simultaneously deriving satisfaction from the dynamic. Your essential being remains constant. The various manifestations of your fundamental existence are subject to alteration. The embodiment of your personal identity is the manifestation through which your intrinsic essence perceives the diverse array of its own manifestations. As previously mentioned, the inseparability of awareness and experience has been stated. Your inherent essence resides in consciousness, and everything within your awareness constitutes the realm of experience. Due to the inseparability of awareness and experience, it can be concluded that you are interconnected with all that exists.

Daily Exercise:

Presented here is an exercise designed to enhance your aptitude in perceiving phenomena beyond the realm of conceptualization:

Please have a seat and carefully observe your surroundings, ensuring that you allocate sufficient time to fully absorb all the details.

Once you are prepared, gently close your eyes and grant yourself the space to unwind.

Envision yourself as an extraterrestrial being hailing from a far-off celestial body, whose objective is to embark upon Earth with the sole purpose of conducting a comprehensive investigation. You possess negligible knowledge regarding this planetary entity, coupled with an absence of previous encounters to reference. Consequently, you lack the capacity to ascertain, discern, scrutinize, or evaluate any aspect of your encounters. Put differently, you are a tabula rasa.

Please open your eyes and take another look at your surroundings. Take your time.

How does your observation experience contrast with your initial observation?

In the event that you failed to discern any disparity between the two observations, it is advisable to continue practicing this exercise until such dissimilarity becomes apparent. Whenever we integrate our thoughts or assessments during the act of observation, we conceptualize the things we perceive. The ability to engage in observation without relying on conceptual thinking is an integral aspect of cultivating mindfulness and being fully present.

Participate In Constructive Behaviors To Yield Favorable Outcomes.

This is the juncture at which numerous adherents of the Law of Attraction encounter their downfall: By neglecting to undertake individualized efforts.

Frequently, our inability to attain what we desire and believe is rightfully ours stems from a lack of effort and dedication. It is imperative that one does not solely depend on mere thoughts to attain their desires. It is probable that thoughtful consideration will lead to the identification of appropriate courses of action. Cogitation serves as the instrument with which your aspirations are formed, however, it is through diligent pursuit that you shall actualize them. Having acquired the knowledge on developing a resilient and optimistic mindset, the next logical progression entails implementing this understanding in practical situations, thereby enabling you to reap the advantages it offers.

Devise a Strategic Plan to Bolster Your Objective

Regardless of your aspirations, it is imperative that you develop a strategic course of action to bolster your objectives. Whether your ambition is to amass a substantial fortune, establish your own enterprise, or simply seek tranquility, it is imperative to undertake actions in order to manifest such aspirations. Unless you take appropriate action in this regard, you will fail to achieve it. Indeed, maintaining a constructive mindset does facilitate the occurrence of favorable experiences. However, if one fixates solely on nurturing positive thoughts without accompanying them with proactive measures, the desired positive outcomes will remain elusive.

Suppose you have been presented with the opportunity to assume a leadership role within your organization for an upcoming project. If you seize this opportunity and effectively guide your team in the project, you stand a chance of securing the promotion you aspire to, thereby advancing towards your objective of augmenting your earnings. Nevertheless, should you choose to reject the prospect or opt to participate half-heartedly without exerting the essential endeavors required to ensure the prosperity of that undertaking, it is evident that you will inevitably fall short of attaining your objective. By virtue of your contemplation, the cosmos has bestowed upon you an opportunity; it now behooves you to seize or squander that prospect. In order to have a significant impact, it is necessary to undertake constructive and purposeful measures.

The endeavor of attaining your objective is facilitated by the presence of a well-structured course of action. An action plan entails a sequence of discrete measures, each contributing to the attainment of the overarching objective. Prominent figures such as Brian Tracy, Tony Robbins, and Jack Canfield not only subscribe to the potential of the Law of Attraction and maintain a positive mental outlook to leverage its effectiveness, but they also excel in formulating strategic initiatives to reinforce their objectives, thereby enabling them to progress towards them with utmost efficiency.

To formulate your course of action, consider your overarching objective and establish a time limit for its achievement. Consider its intrinsic nature and degree of severity, and subsequently contemplate the temporal commitment required for its completion. Establish a pragmatic timeline for its completion, and consequently determine the commencement date for the pursuit of this objective.

Subsequently, break down that objective into intermediate and immediate goals. As an illustration, should the aspiration entail attaining the position of Chief Executive Officer within the organization you currently serve, what specific accomplishments would be requisite to that objective's realization? In this instance, your intermediate objective could entail attaining the position of senior manager within the company, while your immediate objective could involve striving to achieve the designation of branch manager. At present, the pathway to attaining the position of CEO may appear opaque to you. This is precisely why it is imperative for you to direct your attention towards the smaller milestones, as doing so will render the task more feasible and alleviate the sense of being overwhelmed. Consider the immediate objective and devise strategies to attain it. Devise a suitable number of procedural stages to effectively achieve your objective.

Ensure clarity in each step by dividing it into smaller components, thus enhancing its practicability for efficient execution. As soon as you have gained a clearer understanding of how you intend to operationalize your immediate objective, commence your progress by initiating the initial phase and gradually proceed through to the final phase. According to the renowned Martin Luther King Jr., it is not necessary to perceive the entire staircase. Simply initiate the first action."

Executing tasks can frequently be challenging, particularly for individuals unaccustomed to doing so, or those who have been disheartened by the substantiality of their objectives. Nevertheless, by adhering to the subsequent actions, you can effectively conquer your propensity to procrastinate and attain desirable outcomes.

1: Maintain a broad perspective and initiate proceedings promptly.

When the designated time for task completion arrives, please consider the broader perspective. Employ your cognitive faculties to conjure an image of the ultimate fruition of your objective. Utilize the motivation derived from that source to commence the task effectively, without excessive contemplation. If one intends to enhance their swimming abilities with the aim of eventually securing a gold medal in the Olympics, it is advisable to envision their ultimate objective and then proceed to conduct thorough research on reputable swimming institutions to enroll in.

Directing your attention towards the broader scope of your objectives provides the necessary impetus to actively pursue the achievement of your aspirations. Initiating the initial action towards actualizing that objective functions to validate to oneself the commitment to pursue it. Similar qualities tend to attract one another, and subsequently, this propels your enthusiasm to unprecedented levels. It is imperative to consistently evoke a visual representation of your objective whenever the stipulated time for executing your strategy arises, resulting in the gradual cultivation of a habitual routine. Consequently, you will be empowered to engage in purposeful endeavors on a daily basis, eliminating the tendencies of procrastination and discouragement from your repertoire.

2: Venture beyond the confines of familiarity and embrace opportunities for taking calculated risks.

Engaging in purposeful endeavors entails employing every necessary measure to aid in the accomplishment of your objectives. Indeed, it is imperative that you be willing to take calculated risks on occasion and approach challenges with unconventional strategies in order to achieve desirable outcomes. Adhering to societal conventions does not guarantee success in every instance. Indeed, more often than not, it is quite the contrary. If one possesses the audacity to contemplate grand aspirations, one must exhibit the fortitude to undertake substantial gambles necessary to transform those aspirations into tangible achievements.

Unless one ventures beyond the confines of a room and enrolls in flight training, mere daydreams of flying will never materialize. If one holds an aspiration to cultivate an extensive social network, the realization of this ambition remains unattainable in the absence of concerted endeavors to engage with individuals. Attaining your objective frequently necessitates making arduous choices and confronting tasks that you would prefer to avoid. While this may present occasional difficulties, the phrase "whatever it takes" inherently encompasses an unwavering commitment to pursuing the necessary course of action. If one desires to transcend their current state and strive for personal fulfillment, it is crucial to exhibit the audacity required to venture beyond the confines of familiarity and embrace calculated chances.

Please bear in mind, however, that if you find yourself in accordance with the Universal Mind, the course of action you must embark on will not be arduous or disdainful; instead, it will bring you delight as you will be aware that you are striving towards your ultimate objective.

Despite the formulation of a concrete strategy aimed at attaining your objective, it is advisable to remain vigilant and receptive to potential opportunities that may expedite your progress beyond the scope of your devised plan. Ensure that all apparent threats, hazards, and eventualities are thoroughly evaluated to determine the potential for converting them into favorable circumstances. Consider, for instance, the case of Edwin C. Barnes, whose primary aspiration was to establish a career under the employment of Thomas Edison. At that point in time, Edison achieved significant success in his field of invention. Pursuing his burning desire, Barnes met Edison and pleaded with him to train and guide him. Barnes served as an intern under the tutelage of Edison for a duration of 5 years. Over the course of a continuous duration of 5 years, there was a conspicuous absence of any indication or instance presenting itself as a possible avenue through which Barnes could establish a business partnership with Edison. However, despite the circumstances, Barnes remained diligent and dutifully complied with every directive provided by Edison. After the lapse of 5 years, when Edison successfully devised his dictating machine, an auspicious opportunity presented itself to Barnes. Every single one of Edison's current business associates, as well as the salesmen employed under him, unanimously expressed their belief that the dictating machine was destined to fail, advising Edison to abandon the notion of selling it. Barnes, however, thought otherwise. When all individuals relinquished hope in the functioning of the apparatus, Barnes seized the fortuitous moment and resolved to vend it at any expense. He held a strong conviction in his ability to effectively market the machine, and that is precisely what he accomplished. He embarked on a monumental gamble which not only led to his triumph in that endeavor but also facilitated his attainment of such immense prosperity that Edison felt compelled to forge a business partnership with Barnes. If Barnes had lacked faith in his abilities and refrained from undertaking that endeavor, he would have been unable to attain the longed-for success.

Periodically reassess your course of action and contemplate potential modifications to individual steps or phases that could expedite favorable outcomes, even if it entails a measured level of risk.

Refrain from dismissing a novel and daring concept solely based on the belief that it is frivolous, or due to the absence of its implementation by others. Alternatively, conduct an experiment with it and analyze it from various perspectives. With persistent experimentation, you shall ultimately discover an approach that proves efficacious, enabling you to attain the desired outcomes.

Individuals are discouraged from pursuing their own thoughts in the pursuit of truth, even if their ideas deviate slightly from commonly accepted beliefs.

According to John Locke, in his work entitled An Essay Concerning Human Understanding

Encountering formidable circumstances and daring to venture outside of your comfort zone can prove to be a formidable endeavor, yet it is important to bear in mind that significant achievements rarely materialize without effort. Edison conducted approximately 10,000 experiments before ultimately developing an infallible prototype of the electric lightbulb for which he gained renown. If he had not committed those errors, he would not have ultimately discovered the formula that acted as the key to his triumph. You, too, should undertake the same endeavor if you aspire to attain the level of success that you ardently crave. Perseverance is an essential component of the journey towards attaining success, as setbacks and obstacles often prove to be inevitable.

3: Engage in Reciprocity

"The philanthropic act is quintessential to the art of existence." - Tony Robbins

It may astound you to discover that the individuals endowed with immense wealth rank among the most magnanimous members of our global community. At present, it is conceivable that the initial thought that might arise in your mind is, "Indeed, Gabriele, they are capable of exhibiting generosity as a result of their substantial financial resources." Undeniably, this assertion holds true. However, it is important to note that similar entities tend to gravitate towards one another. When individuals engage in selfless and generous acts, they are able to tap into the power of the universe, allowing it to reciprocate their contributions abundantly and surpassingly. Indeed, how can one offer something if they are not receiving an increase in return? It is required to do so in accordance with legal mandates. Identify a philanthropic organization that resonates with you and donate any amount you are able to, as frequently as possible. Not only will you experience a significant increase in blessings, but the profound sense of contentment that accompanies such acts will also elevate your frequency to a remarkable extent.

This principle extends beyond mere wealth and encompasses the realization of objectives pertaining to health, love, relationships, happiness, and peace as well. In order to manifest any desired aspect in your life, it is imperative that you undertake a reciprocal action. As an example, if one desires to attain affection from others, they must first demonstrate affection to those in their vicinity.

Engage in meaningful interactions with cherished individuals; demonstrate genuine curiosity in their lives; convey affectionate emotions towards them; and initiate contact to bestow your fondness upon them. Your diligent contributions shall undeniably be recognized, and you will inevitably attract an abundance of affection that surpasses all expectations. Want to experience happiness? Perform an action on behalf of an individual while being cognizant of the fact that it will undoubtedly elicit joy in them. You will encounter immediate felicity.

As you reflect upon the aforementioned points and the content presented in the preceding chapters, it is imperative to articulate a few additional matters in order to fully harness the potential of the Law. Initially, it is imperative to exercise caution and mindfulness in regards to one's thoughts, emotions, and actions, ensuring that they correspond harmoniously with one's intentions and planned course of action, thereby optimizing the likelihood of achieving one's objective.

Additionally, it is imperative to prioritize your own interests and adopt a self-centered approach, in order to concentrate on enhancing your personal development as a primary focus. You can only transition to being selfless and supporting those around you once you have enhanced yourself, refined your attributes, and achieved the persona you aspire to. This situation is rather ironic, particularly given our earlier discourse on the subject of generosity, isn't it?

Establishing Your Vision

A vision is an influential and potent notion. It conveys a meaning that transcends mere knowledge of one's destination, objectives, or the means to achieve them. Your vision encapsulates your desired future state, serving as a blueprint that outlines your long-term aspirations and delineates the methods by which you will achieve them, leveraging your current skills, knowledge, and resources. It serves as a source of motivation and inspiration. The possession of a vision holds greater significance than the pursuit of a goal. Indeed, the majority of objectives fail to fulfill their intended purpose unless they are preceded by a visionary perspective. While concrete goals may exist, their efficacy is contingent upon their alignment with a broader framework and their ability to contribute to an overarching objective. Without this holistic approach, these goals may lack the necessary strength to be successfully pursued.

Having a clear understanding of your vision can enable you to surmount challenges and attain achievements that might otherwise have been beyond your grasp. Lacking a clear life purpose, it becomes effortless to be derailed by the routine of daily existence and make susceptible to falling behind, particularly concerning the endeavors to manifest desired outcomes. The presence of a clear vision enables one to undertake the requisite measures to achieve their objective, as it serves as a constant reminder to cultivate positive thoughts and actively embody these concepts every day. The possession of a well-defined vision also serves to instill a sense of inspiration, prompting one to be willing to make the requisite sacrifices necessary for the realization of said vision. These sacrifices may encompass forgoing social engagements in favor of ensuring adequate rest prior to significant upcoming events, or establishing firm boundaries with those whose guiding principles are incongruent with one's own. Having a clear vision facilitates concentration and enables one to be fully present, thereby enhancing the ability to manifest the most treasured aspects of one's life.

Posessing a vision is akin to possessing a navigational guide. In the absence of a well-defined plan or a set of principles that harmonize with your overarching vision, one can readily stray from the intended path and regress into the aforementioned pattern of pessimism.

The foundation of your vision consists of two key elements, with the first being values. Merely having a vision is insufficient. You are required to consistently uphold and implement it based on your principles on a daily basis. Your actions and decision-making should be guided by your principles and beliefs. For instance, in what do you place the highest degree of belief? What is your perception of the most significant aspect of life? Might you prioritize integrity and loyalty over other factors? Alternatively, do you believe that diligent effort and maintaining a strong focus on one's career objectives are vital tenets to abide by? By adhering to these principles, you will be steered on the path of your manifestational journey.

When one experiences a sense of discord or a lack of self-respect, it becomes apparent that their actions are not in alignment with their core values. Please consider this suggestion and trust your own intuition - you are currently projecting a different energy than what you wish to attract. Redirect yourself back onto the correct path and rely on your instincts. You possess the greatest understanding of your own self.

The following element pertains to your objective or intention. This is the factor that propels you towards your envisioned life, as it serves as the source of inspiration, compelling you to stay steadfast on the correct trajectory. This purpose pertains to the overarching "why", or the underlying rationale behind each and every undertaken action. Would you be interested in assisting a substantial number of individuals to enhance their quality of life? Would you desire a sense of fulfillment as you age? Alternatively, you may desire to reside in constant company of your loved ones and choose to embrace each passing day as it unfolds before you. The purpose you possess must possess such fortitude that it steadfastly guides your every action, even during times of uncertainty. Maybe you want to start traveling every single month and want to live a nomadic lifestyle, or perhaps you want to live a childless life and live by your own rules. The fervor that you experience towards the idealized depiction of your "optimal existence" should serve as the foundation for determining your true purpose. Do not be alarmed by potential fluctuations – they are highly probable! As you encounter diverging circumstances and interact with varied individuals, you might discover a corresponding evolution in your purpose, and rest assured, this is entirely acceptable.

Every day, prioritize your actions towards progressing towards your ultimate purpose. Recognize the aspects requiring modification in your lifestyle to attain your goals and substitute unfavorable behaviors with positive ones. For instance, if your priority is traveling and financial savings are crucial, limit your outings to one night per week instead of the current frequency of two nights. To achieve business growth, it is imperative to explore potential cost reduction opportunities and meticulously consider personal decisions that might impede this forward momentum. A vision statement, such as "I aspire to lead a life of abundance" or "My goal is to make a positive impact on others," holds significance only when it is accompanied by a genuine commitment to devote effort towards it every morning upon awakening. Possessing a clearly defined vision statement and actively embodying it in every facet of one's existence engenders a potent sense of affirmation, bestowing a sense of direction and significance.

Regarding the topic of vision statements, this particular phase can be considered as the subsequent sub-component within your manifestation procedure. After gaining a comprehensive understanding of your vision, you should be capable of succinctly summarizing it in a single sentence. Crafting a vision statement assumes utmost significance in the formation and progression of one's existence. If one lacks the ability to envision oneself at the conclusion of their endeavors, it becomes difficult to muster the necessary drive to strive for achievement. A vision statement serves as a strategic tool for establishing a structured framework governing your self-perception and the desired outcomes you seek to achieve through your pursuits. It may possess brevity; however, it ought to exemplify clarity and conciseness. This is an item that you may also incorporate into your vision board, a topic we will explore further in the third phase of our discussion.

Cease Desiring; Commence Possessing.

If one is able to perceive it, they will eventually witness it. You must identify a method of comforting yourself with the understanding that if you are able to perceive it, then it is within reach and can be achieved. This mode of receptivity simply implies that you are in the process of receiving something. You exert an impact on that state of receptivity by imparting impetus to a thought or emotion.

If you possess an awareness of your emotive state and hold a certain affinity towards that state, direct your attention in its direction. One has the ability to elevate any notion of lesser significance by directing their attention towards it, thereby bestowing it with significant importance, ultimately resulting in its materialization in the present moment. Remember, you are God.

One could apply this approach to any item or matter of significance. This exemplifies the immense strength of the cosmos that is presently aligned in your favor. This exemplifies the profound influence of the concentrated source energy that is currently cooperating with you. You have an abundance of resources readily available to you; within you lies the potent force that gives rise to entire universes.

You have the potential to achieve, accomplish, or possess anything, but it is essential to compartmentalize your endeavors in such a manner that reinforces your awareness of your progress. Select something of significance to you and make a deliberate choice to concentrate on it until you can demonstrate personal improvement within a single day.

In the span of a single day, witness the evolution of the subject's significance, moving from mere discussion to a sense of satisfaction, culminating in an exhilarating surge of enthusiasm. Allow that sense of anticipation to intensify until it materializes.

In fact, it is a frequent occurrence in your everyday activities. You may be unaware of your actions and therefore fail to acknowledge or evaluate them, whether positively or negatively. Thus, select any subject matter of your choice, engage in thoughtful contemplation, allow your emotions to gather strength and intensity around said subject, and concentrate unwaveringly with persistence.

Consider, what would be the emotional and psychological impact of possessing that item, visiting that location, or achieving that goal. Indulge in that sentiment and refrain from relinquishing it.

One might pose the question, for instance, "In what manner can the funds be extracted from the vortex and deposited into the bank?"

When can I anticipate its arrival?

One cannot discuss the unpleasant aspects of the drought and expect it to result in rainfall; one cannot acknowledge the absence of something and magically have that absence filled.

It is imperative that you endeavor to alter your perspective such that you permit the gradual gathering of momentum within the vortex. The resonance you are extending must align with the vibrational frequency associated with the desired manifestation.

Are you requesting to have funds deposited into your bank account? Consider reflecting upon the following query: "Does my mindset and emotional state align with the vibrational frequency of wealth, affluence, abundance, comfort, and prosperity, rather than dwelling on the challenges of saving money, the continuous outflow of funds, and the accumulation of bills?"

You must cultivate within yourself the ability to experience the profound satisfaction stemming from the realization that what you desire has already manifested. Have faith in your divine existence and consider that the object of your pursuit has already come into fruition, for it has already come to pass.

There is no requirement for you to obtain anyone's permission, approval, guidance, or consent in granting yourself whatever it is that you desire. Indulge in whatever you aspire to entirely at your own discretion. Effortlessly cultivate the impetus surrounding the presence of your desired outcome and persist unwaveringly, as your desired outcome is likewise earnestly in pursuit of you.

Fostering A Financial Outlook

It is imperative that you promptly dismiss from your memory any adverse remarks or criticisms that may have been imparted to you over the course of your life. You possess the inherent worthiness to attain the highest quality of life imaginable and have the capacity to accomplish any desired goal. You are deserving of everything that you desire. Many individuals express the sentiment that they do not believe they are deserving of the two-story farmhouse they have envisioned since their youth, the vintage '69 Corvette, the promotion they have been aspiring to, and the financial success they desire.

You are deserving of all that you aspire to attain. Given your existence, you can avail yourself of the boundless wealth of opportunities that life has to offer. The corporations, media entities, religious establishments, and various institutions have effectively propagated the notion that we fail to meet the required standard. It is possible that you may have begun to entertain the notion that you possess inadequate abilities or qualities. Perhaps you believe that you lack the deserving qualities. You may be under the impression that your level of intelligence is inadequate. Due to the substantial errors that you have made in the past, it is deemed necessary to withhold certain privileges such as freedom, success, abundance, and joy that are typically available to individuals who have not experienced similar setbacks. This is primarily attributed to the past transgressions you have committed, the sins you have carried, the manner in which you were raised, or simply due to the occurrence of a mistake.

It is possible that you may hold the belief that your lower limbs possess an insufficient girth or that your buttocks exhibit a disproportionate size. You may hold the belief that you lack the necessary competence or intellect. One might perceive oneself as lacking a strong memory. This is entirely baseless and unsubstantiated. It has been meticulously orchestrated to manipulate our behavior via the media, institutions, and religious systems, compelling us to purchase their goods, despite their lack of necessity and inherent insignificance, save for a momentary gratification that swiftly dissipates. This can be regarded as a means of exerting social influence and regulation.

If one does not possess the belief in their own intellectual prowess and self-worth, their autonomy will be subjugated. I am endeavoring to convey to you that you possess inherent value and merit. So say this to yourself, "I am worthy of everything I desire." Say it again and again and again. It is imperative that this knowledge becomes deeply embedded within your cognition. Repeat the affirmation, "I possess inherent worthiness to attain all that I aspire to."

This isn't anything new. This aims to charm and attract your attention. You unequivocally merit each and every thing you aspire for. Individuals who attain notable accomplishments and generate extraordinary creations possess a self-belief in their deservingness to attain such successes. They do not possess any superior qualities or attributes in comparison to yourself. They do not possess any superior qualities compared to others. We are all worthy. Each and every one of us is worthy of it.

Each of us is entitled to the highest quality of life achievable. Each individual is entitled to experience joy and contentment in their lives. Each of us is entitled to be treated with dignity and consideration by others. You deserve it, too. This implies that you have the right to decline and remove individuals from your life who may not be offering the level of support that you are entitled to. This could imply that you will have to decline various commitments. This could imply that it may be necessary to assert your desires, as they rightfully belong to you. If one is deserving of everything they have ever desired, if one possesses the requisite worthiness and qualifications for their aspirations, and if one is adequately prepared, then there remains no further need for preparation. There is no requirement for the purification of one's transgressions or the cleansing of one's energy, as all necessary actions have already been carried out. What would you do?

What creations would you bring into existence? What actions would you undertake in the forthcoming year to ensure that it becomes the utmost gratifying and prosperous year of your existence? What are the things that you truly merit? What are your aspirations and objectives for yourself, your community, and your family? What?

If there exist no further requirements for achieving worthiness, ascending to a higher energetic state, or purging the ingrained processes of your subconsciousness? If one were to be liberated from the influences of purported acquaintances, the offensive remarks proffered by one's superiors, the disparaging remarks expressed by one's acquaintances, and the undertones of guidance imparted by educators, if these factors were to inexplicably dissipate, what course of action would one diligently pursue?

Allow me to reaffirm the notion that you possess the inherent worthiness to attain everything you desire.

Simply train your subconscious mind to believe in your own worthiness of abundance and success. You must discard any unfounded notions that undermine your sense of competence, worth, or intelligence. You must expunge those thoughts from your memory. You are not obliged to accept any negativity. You need not tolerate any disrespectful behavior from anyone. You are entitled to pursue your desires and navigate life with serenity and contentment, crafting an existence aligned with your true aspirations, free from perceptions of your self-worth imposed by external influences.

You are deserving of a truly remarkable life, and I wish to affirm that you possess inherent worth. I am present to provide you with a positive affirmation that it is advisable to reiterate to yourself frequently throughout the day.

I am entitled to all that I aspire for. I am deserving of ample quantities of all that I aspire to, including prosperity, fulfillment, joy, and affection. I deserve it. I am deserving of all that I aspire to attain."

Now, proceed forthwith with the newfound audacity and assurance that you possess. Stride confidently towards your aspirations and observe the universe's reciprocal reaction. Assert your rightful entitlement and just due. We reside within a world that is characterized by a profusion of resources and boundless possibilities. Sufficient opportunities exist for each individual to partake in a state of abundance, achievement, autonomy, affection, and elation that aligns with our desires.

Exhibiting Consciousness Of Adverse Patterns And Detrimental Beliefs

Cogitation gives rise to Convictions and Convictions give rise to Schemes. Patterns give rise to conduct, and conduct determines one's ultimate fate. In instances when an unfavorable thought arises and elicits a sense of immobilization, astonishment, apprehension, remorse, or any adverse mental state, it is imperative to diligently assign a descriptive term to the thought and affix it with a identifier. By employing this method, you are effectively ensuring the detection and apprehension of this specific matter, ultimately preparing it for removal from your system.

FOR INSTANCE: While engrossed in a task, one may unexpectedly experience a distressing recollection of a previous event involving some form of wrongdoing inflicted upon oneself. Presently, this notion is endeavoring to seize your attention towards the errant aspects. This notion seeks the attainment of fairness and equity. Henceforth, you may designate this concept as "Thoughts pertaining to Injustice."

When imbued with a distinct designation, one inevitably evokes latent or concealed impressions of inequity that had previously resided inert within their energetic being. By bestowing a name upon it, one materializes its existence and assumes authoritative control over it. You have taken full ownership, and henceforth, the course of action you undertake lies entirely in your hands. One may effectively communicate the instruction "Cease all contemplation of grievances at this present moment."

➤ You are permitted to diligently execute this directive for an extended duration, until such time that it imparts upon you a sensation and perception of being independent from the dominating influence of this thought. Upon its release, you shall experience the onset of yawning or drowsiness. This phenomenon is typically indicative of the dissipation of energy.

➢ The hard sign of energy release is diarrhea, fever, headache, runny nose or depression. In the event that the blockage possesses significant weight, harboring intense negative emotions and emanating low vibrational energy, its subsequent release may prove arduous, potentially leading to feelings of discomfort and physical distress.

And that is precisely the reason why one would be reluctant to alleviate the obstruction, as it is widely known to be a source of great anguish. However, retaining the block is associated with detrimental consequences, as it tends to attract unfavorable relationships and circumstances that inflict distress and unease.

➤ If you encounter such a circumstance where you

perceive the thoughts to be burdensome and distressing, you have the option of employing the terms 'NEUTRALIZE,' 'DEFUSE,' 'DEACTIVATE,' 'BANISH,' or 'TRANSMUTE' in order to alter the energy of the thoughts into a state that is neutral and innocuous.

The instructions for the Pendulum Commands are outlined below:

I urge for the complete eradication and withdrawal

of all perceptions of injustice from my being at this moment."

Eliminate and dispel any lingering thoughts of failure from my being immediately."

Eliminate and free my mind from any thoughts of inadequacy at this present moment."

Eliminate and dismiss all thoughts of victimization from my mind at this moment"

I kindly request that all apprehensive thoughts be eradicated and freed from my energetic sphere at this very moment."

I implore the immediate removal and liberation of all perturbing thoughts from my existence at this moment.

Cease and relinquish all distressing thoughts pertaining to previous occurrences at this present moment.

I request for the cessation and liberation of all negative thoughts stemming from previous experiences."

Mitigate and relinquish any and all feelings of shame associated with my past errors at this moment"

I kindly request that any embarrassing thoughts concerning my past mistakes be diffused and released at this moment.

Visualization: Experience The Resonance Of Your Desires.

Suppose I were to inform you that a considerable portion of the accomplishments you have achieved in your life can be attributed to the practice of partial visualization? These notions do not simply spontaneously arise in one's mind and somehow imbue motivation. Due to some unknown cause, you were able to sustain your enthusiasm or dedication towards your project, leading to the successful alignment of circumstances. You have successfully accomplished your objectives.

The majority of individuals possess the capacity to accomplish this task; however, in order to realize your utmost aspirations and transform them into tangible results, one must exhibit unwavering commitment in following through with this procedure. This section is often a point of difficulty for many individuals.

While you can count on them to get it right at least part of the time, when it comes to consistent success, most find it hard. One primary factor contributing to this phenomenon is our tendency to underestimate the potential of visualization. It serves as an indispensable instrument for transforming fleeting thoughts and bringing them to fruition.

Why does visualization work?

It is imperative to bear in mind that individuals frequently conceive notions. Many of these are instigated by the projects that we are presently engaged in. We have discovered a more effective method for accomplishing tasks. Once we identify specific patterns through our actions, we proceed to establish connections between different data points. In light of this, one can observe that with sufficient repetition, the mind will inevitably generate efficient strategies. Each individual possesses an innate brilliance that can be harnessed. In due time, we will inevitably discover means to enhance our efficiency in our customary undertakings.

However, our ability to execute such tasks does not necessarily imply that we actually carry them out. A lot of people are also smart enough to realize that, often, in most offices and factory floors throughout the United States, the reward for coming up with faster ways to do work is yet more work. According to the age-old adage, any act of benevolence does not go unrewarded. However, every one of us possesses this capacity.

The issue lies in the ephemerality of many of these ideas. We devise expedient workarounds or resolutions, yet ultimately, they slip from our recollection. The majority of these circumstances stem from our occasional utilization of these methods, or our insistence on pursuing innovation and finding expedited solutions when faced with adversity. Upon the dissipation of such urgency or challenge, we revert to our customary modus operandi. Hence, concepts arise and dissipate.

The unfortunate aspect lies in the fact that visualization offers the opportunity to direct one's attention towards their objectives, thereby channeling a substantial amount of their cognitive and emotional faculties towards the actualization of said goals. This strategy is an indispensable resource that must be harnessed in order to attain enduring prosperity. It is imperative to depend on it should you wish to consistently dedicate effort towards your ambitious objectives.

As previously stated in this literary work, life ensues during the process of formulating alternate arrangements. You may possess an array of clearly delineated strategies, frameworks, and blueprints concerning the trajectory you desire for your life. It is highly probable that you have invested a significant duration of time and exerted substantial effort in compiling those proposals. However, it is highly unlikely that such outcomes will materialize unless you consistently dedicate efforts towards them. If they fail to do so, it is highly likely that you will experience a sense of disappointment.

The manifestation of your objectives and aspirations does not entirely align with your initial perception of them. Significant discrepancies emerged during the translation process as your initial objective evolved into a tangible manifestation. Visualizations increase the likelihood that the objective you strive for will manifest as your actual outcome.

The secret to visualization

In numerous planning circles and workgroups, the advent of visualization often elicits skepticism from certain individuals. It is relatively effortless to engage in light-hearted banter regarding a process in which one simply constructs a hypothetical existence. It appears reminiscent of indulging in idle fantasies or conjuring fanciful ideas that hold no practical relevance. However, visualization encompasses a multitude of aspects beyond merely picturing the presence of a desired outcome.

It is of paramount importance to position oneself in close proximity to the envisioned outcome that one desires to materialize. Put simply, you need to establish an emotional investment in what you are observing. One cannot simply conceptualize an alternate version of the actuality they are experiencing and regard it as a mere fictional motion picture.

Whilst viewing a film, one is cognizant of the fact that they did not partake in the scriptwriting or production processes. You do not perceive yourself in the roles of director or actor. You are merely a passive participant in this endeavor. Therefore, after meticulously choosing your desired movie to stream on the Netflix platform, you leisurely recline in the plush confines of your chair, allowing the film to unfold seamlessly before your eyes.

It constitutes a discourse conducted unilaterally, with pre-recorded amusement. Your feedback is not obligatory. One's only possible recourse is to discern an emotional response to the situation at hand, yet ultimately one does not hold decision-making authority. Ultimately, you were not the author of the script. You do not hold the position of the director.

It constitutes an exceedingly passive mode of amusement, characterized by unidirectional engagement. The individuals responsible for the creation of this movie, including the writer, director, producer, actors, and others, have contributed their efforts. It is now your sole responsibility to determine your personal preference towards it. Your sole contribution consisted of remaining seated and passively observing the creations presented to you. This action does not constitute visualization.

By visualizing your goals, you establish a reciprocal feedback mechanism with the objective you have defined for yourself. Upon envisioning oneself residing in said alternative reality, one's perception becomes attuned to intricate particulars. These particulars are dissimilar to those depicted in a film. One can observe the presence of a plot loophole, yet its rectification remains significantly limited. In light of the aforementioned circumstances, it is pertinent to note that the video had already been produced. Your only course of action is to observe. The aforementioned does not apply to visualization.

One of the most powerful advantages of visualization is the opportunity to effectively experience an alternate reality. You begin to perceive these intricate particulars and come to the realization that you possess authority over your own perspective. You have the ability to input the necessary data. Additionally, one can identify contradictory information and resolve any inconsistencies. Crucially, the act of visualizing engenders an emotional commitment to the ongoing events.

It exerts a substantial influence on both your being and emotional state. Then, change your vision. You generate a reciprocal feedback mechanism. This heightened level of involvement facilitates the ability to immerse oneself in an alternate reality through emotional experiences, while concurrently permitting that vision to impact one's immediate sentiments. Not only are you afforded the opportunity to fully immerse yourself in an alternative perception of reality, owing to your deep emotional involvement, but it also engenders an uncanny sense of realism.

Please be reminded that when mental images appear in your mind, they are typically devoid of emotional neutrality. There exist discrete visual representations that elicit feelings of joy or nostalgia. Others upset you. When engaging in the practice of visualization, the identical dynamics come into play. As one delves into this cognitive realm, they position themselves to absorb their fervor while operating with a heightened sense of emotional impetuosity.

The stronger your ability to envision your aspirations becomes, the more pronounced your sensory perceptions of sight, sound, touch, taste, and smell become. It is indeed genuine, despite its existence being confined solely within your consciousness. Fortunately, none of the structures that currently surround you were in existence prior to this point. It required the conceptualization of an architect to envision those formations within their cognitive faculties, prior to transposing them onto architectural blueprints.

The above statement is equally relevant in your case. Within your mind, you possess notions that you conscientiously invest yourself in within this alternate realm, wherein lies the depiction of your ambitious aspirations in life. You inhabit a distinct location, and your persona has undergone a transformation.

When engaging in this action, you alter the vibrational frequencies that you emit into the cosmos. It attains a greater level of precision as it incorporates your envisioned future outcomes. It does not attempt to comprehend or rationalize nor does it exhibit bewilderment or detachment from reality. Your thoughts do not engage in cyclical or erratic patterns. When engaging in visualization, one is able to perceive a distinct, sharp, and striking mental representation of the desired outcome.

Consequently, by diligently cultivating your vibrational energy in this manner, the messages that you transmit into the cosmos become more precisely delineated. Given your current emotional involvement, there is no absence of connection. There exists a complete alignment between your genuine aspirations and the innermost depths of your heart.

Occasionally, when you introspect and delve into your thoughts, you might experience uncertainty or perceive it as a futile allocation of your time. Such occurrences are absent in this context as your emotional involvement and dedication to the overarching vision of your ultimate reality are apparent. Permit yourself to fully immerse in the visual depiction by engaging all of your senses.

Generally, when individuals mention the term "visualization," they are frequently alluding to the notion of sensory perception. To truly evoke a profound and enduring level of emotional commitment to the alternative vision you hold for your future, it is imperative that you extend your efforts beyond the aforementioned approach and also engage your other sensory faculties. What range of emotions do you anticipate experiencing upon embarking upon the envisioned future lifestyle?

Advantages of Engaging in Daily Affirmations

Daily affirmations encompass constructive declarations that individuals repetitively and consistently address to themselves each day. These statements have been purposefully crafted to invoke a sense of empowerment and inspiration, directed towards specific objectives or intentions. The utilization of daily affirmations is thought to offer various potential advantages, encompassing:

Improving self-esteem and self-confidence. Through the practice of affirming positive statements about oneself on a consistent basis, there exists the potential to augment one's self-esteem and self-assurance. This can assist individuals in fostering a greater sense of self-efficacy and enable them to actively pursue their objectives.

Manifesting goals and intentions. Through the deliberate practice of directing our attention towards particular objectives or aspirations using regular affirmations, it is conceivable that we can materialize these longings in the physical realm. This can assist individuals in realizing their objectives and aspirations.

Reducing stress and anxiety. Regularly practicing positive self-statements can assist in reframing detrimental thoughts and emotions, ultimately mitigating the levels of stress and anxiety experienced. Through the cultivation of positive statements and beliefs, individuals have the potential to attain heightened tranquility and serenity in their day-to-day existence.

Improving overall well-being. The utilization of daily affirmations has been correlated with enhanced general state of well-being. Through the cultivation of optimistic thoughts and convictions, individuals have the potential to enhance their mental and emotional well-being, ultimately experiencing increased contentment and fulfillment in their lives.

In general, the utilization of daily affirmations presents various possibilities for individuals to enhance their mental and emotional welfare, as well as triumphantly attain their objectives and ambitions.

Strategies For Manifesting Joy And Happiness

Every individual seeks to partake in the pursuit of joy and contentment throughout their lifetime. All individuals aspire to encounter profound happiness and enduring sentiments of satisfaction. Fortunately, one can utilize the principle of the law of attraction to manifest a multitude of manifestations, including but not limited to the acquisition of contentment and delight. Here are the steps on how to use the law of attraction to manifest unlimited joy and happiness in your life:

- Make the conscious decision to pursue happiness. or - Resolve to prioritize your own happiness. Please ensure to record that objective and have faith in your ability to accomplish it.

Engage in introspection and dedicate a moment to contemplate the aspects that bring joy to your life. Consider recollecting your most joyous and amusing reminiscences, while consciously steering clear of any somber ones. In the event that you happen to find your mind preoccupied with contemplations concerning the demise of a close acquaintance or a sorrowful incident encountered in your professional life, expeditiously substitute those ruminations with a constructive and enjoyable idea. Consider the instances when you were leisurely engaged in a vacation alongside your family, or when you achieved a desired advancement in your employment that closely aligned with your professional aspirations. Optimistic and affirmative thoughts possess the ability to promptly generate a sense of well-being.

Release yourself from the burdens of your emotional past. Every individual carries emotional burdens that hinder their pursuit of a fulfilling and deservedly joyful existence. By relinquishing your emotional burdens, releasing all remorse, and granting yourself forgiveness for the errors and poor choices you have made throughout your life, attaining happiness becomes more attainable. Take time to make an emotional inventory and carefully examine all the negative emotions that are holding you back – guilt, anger, shame, and jealousy.

- Show mercy towards those who have committed grievous actions against you. Resentment has the capacity to inflict a powerful blow to one's sense of joy and happiness. It is important to comprehend that forgiveness can primarily be advantageous for your own well-being, as it enables you to progress and embrace the abundance of experiences life presents. Has your partner engaged in infidelity? Did your parents exhibit any form of parental neglect during your formative years? Is your superior not behaving justly towards you? Did you experience instances of bullying during your time at work and school? Resentment is a widely prevalent venom that individuals imbibe regularly. When one liberates oneself from feelings of resentment, one gains the freedom to lead a life filled with happiness and bliss.

- Pardon yourself and relinquish any lingering detrimental emotions, such as shame and guilt. - Grant yourself forgiveness and release any residual negative sentiments, such as shame and guilt. - Absolve yourself and liberate yourself from any lingering adverse emotions, such as shame and guilt. - Excuse yourself and free yourself from any remaining detrimental feelings, such as shame and guilt. In the event that you have committed grievous actions or acts of misconduct in the past, it is of utmost importance to grant oneself forgiveness and acknowledge that perfection is unattainable. Everybody makes mistakes.

Surround yourself with individuals who exude positivity and contentment. According to the principle of the law of attraction, similar entities tend to be drawn to one another. In order to experience a life filled with happiness and joy, it is imperative to associate oneself with individuals who possess an unwavering and optimistic perspective on existence. It can be challenging to experience happiness when one is consistently surrounded by individuals who incessantly voice complaints about various matters.

- Dedicate a moment to visualizing contentment. - Allocate some time to mentally envisioning joy. - Set aside a portion of your day to imagine feelings of bliss. - Invest effort into picturing a state of happiness. If you have been experiencing prolonged periods of sadness or depression, it is important to allocate time for actively envisioning a state of happiness. Upon awakening each day, endeavor to envision a state of contentment and bliss permeating your existence. Envision oneself engaging in joyous moments, experiencing delight, and reveling in an overwhelming sense of happiness. Envision yourself wearing a constant smile, relishing each and every moment.

Select images depicting individuals expressing joy and affix them onto your inspirational board. Should you have been enduring profound sadness or depression over an extended duration, it becomes arduous for you to envisage contentment. Individuals who have endured prolonged episodes of depression are prone to experiencing difficulty in recalling or recognizing the sensations and manifestations of happiness. The images will assist in visually perceiving the sensations of joy and happiness.

- Express gratitude. Expressing gratitude is the most expeditious path to achieving contentment. When one expresses gratitude for the numerous positive elements and blessings they have received, it becomes less challenging for them to cultivate a state of contentment and happiness. Dedicate a moment to find solace in a tranquil setting, and meticulously compose a comprehensive list of all the things that elicit sentiments of gratitude within you. You will promptly observe a discernible enhancement in your overall state of wellbeing.

- Exemplify and embody happiness as a role model. In order to cultivate an atmosphere of happiness and joy, it is recommended to propagate positive energy and assume the role of a goodwill ambassador for happiness. Promote feelings of joy and happiness while actively endeavoring to uplift individuals who experience sadness and depression. Frequently engage in humor and elicit laughter from individuals regularly. Please be mindful that whatever you contribute to the world will eventually be reciprocated. If one disseminates happiness and positive energy, they will encounter a heightened sense of joy and bliss in their existence.

Cultivate a Favorable Mental Attitude: Harnessing the Power of Mind, Physique, and Spirit

As previously elucidated in the introductory section, it is imperative to align the frequency of your radio device with that of your preferred radio program, in order to facilitate the listening experience. We also operate in a similar manner, and in order to accomplish our objectives through manifestation, it is imperative that we acquire the necessary skills to align our mind, body, and psyche towards positive aspirations. In the present day, individuals are excessively engrossed in material possessions to the extent that they are no longer able to derive fulfillment from their human existence. Individuals attribute their lack of wealth and happiness, in comparison to those residing in their vicinity, to divine negligence. This notion becomes entrenched within their subconscious, eliciting feelings of sadness, prompting them to immerse themselves in profound sorrow and grief. By adopting this approach, we effectively align our mental and physical state with detrimental frequencies, leading to a life defined by suffering and sorrow. The contemporary society in which we currently reside is an artificial construct shaped by the actions of human beings. In the early stages of human existence within this Universe, the absence of poverty, sorrow, and grief was evident. During that period, the advent of currency had not yet taken place, a pivotal factor responsible for the oscillation between joy and sorrow. Subsequently, our predecessors acquired knowledge in the cultivation of crops, culinary practices, and ultimately, pioneered the development of precious metals such as gold, diamond, and silver. Previously, they encountered challenges in exchanging their possessions, such as the requirement of offering three sheep in exchange for a single cow. However, with the inception of valuable adornments such as gold and silver, this practice was streamlined, hence

151

enabling individuals to execute exchanges seamlessly by trading commensurate amounts of gold or silver. As the passage of time ensued, humanity made significant technological advancements. We became deeply entrenched in the pursuit of accumulating wealth, engrossed in a frenetic cycle of earning and consumption, all the while losing sight of the fundamental essence that drives our existence as human beings—our shared humanity.

The majority of individuals residing in the present era hold the belief that material wealth is of paramount importance. This line of thinking presents itself as a prevalent hindrance when it comes to cultivating a harmonious alignment between our mental and physical faculties in pursuit of favorable ambitions. Money was initially conceived to facilitate the transactional process, though it is important to note that it is not money per se, but rather the vibrations it embodies, that prove advantageous. In order to cultivate a receptive mindset for positive energy, it is imperative to engage in positive thinking. Have you ever witnessed the sight of yogis stationed in elevated regions of the Himalayas, clad in a single garment, or the monks who reside in the renowned monastic institutions in close proximity to the Himalayas? You have, at the very least, observed them through televised or recorded visual media. If your answer is in the affirmative, you would have come to the realization that these yogis possess an exceptionally refined state of mind, physique, and inner being. One would have observed the presence of a distinct luminosity adorning their countenance. These practitioners of yoga attune their minds, divesting themselves of material possessions, resulting in the luminous radiance and inner strength apparent in both their mental and physical states. However, it would be impractical for individuals with ordinary lives encompassing multiple relationships, professional pursuits, and material possessions to embark on a journey to the Himalayas in pursuit of uncovering the genuine depths of mental and physical capabilities. What measures can be taken to optimize the functioning of our mind and body?

I would recommend individuals refrain from regarding currency solely as money in order to enhance their personal development. Indeed, your comprehension is accurate – consider money as a resonance of frequency rather than a concrete means for all things. One prevalent error individuals often make when sharpening their mental faculties is perceiving money as a tangible asset capable of fulfilling all needs and desires. Consider the notion that while monetary pursuits may not be your primary focus, they nonetheless play a crucial role in attaining various forms of contentment and fulfillment in your existence. We should endeavor to associate wealth with a specific brand of contentment, rather than solely its capacity for material acquisition. In the present context, monetary assets possess the capability to procure various resources on your behalf. It is therefore advisable to embrace a constructive mindset when envisioning the possession of such resources. For instance, consider the scenario wherein you possess a high-end automobile, and subsequently endeavor to establish a profound connection between your physical and mental state, thereby immersing yourself in the experience of holding a luxury vehicle. Envision the aromatic ambiance of the air conditioning and opulent furnishings of your high-end vehicle, and contemplate the experience of actually being in the driver's seat. However, it is imperative to approach this exercise with a sanguine mindset, devoid of any apprehension. If you give consideration to your neighbor's automobile while contemplating the ownership of a vehicle, you will fail to align your thoughts and physique with the genuine sensation of possessing a high-end car. One might have surmised that - "This idea lacks coherence as I possess this automobile exclusively in my dreams, whereas its physical manifestation occurs in my neighbor's possession. When one associates their emotions with such a negative notion, their alignment with that specific vibrational frequency is severed, ultimately impeding the attainment of their desires." Thus, it is recommended that one adopts a mindset characterized by optimism and positivity prior to embarking upon the practice of manifestation.

The Play of Creation

The entirety of existence revolves around the principle of the law of attraction, whereby we observe and let go of the intricate dynamics of the human ego.

The process of creation is uncomplicated and direct. All that you have brought about thus far has been attained effortlessly. As one begins to invest in a task diligently, they convey to the universe their dissatisfaction with their current state. This engenders discord in the process of your manifestation. In the forthcoming chapters, we shall extensively delve into numerous facets of manifestation. However, in order to construct something in accordance with our desires, a robust foundation is imperative for providing sustenance.

This chapter will serve as a firm cornerstone, providing you with a thorough understanding of the concept of the law of attraction and the mechanics behind manifestation. A prevalent error committed by nearly every practitioner is their attempt to outwit the universe. Merely holding faith in or envisioning something for a brief period does not ascertain its truth or materialization. Visualizations will come to fruition solely upon being prepared to receive the object of your visualization, and upon executing it with the appropriate intent or sentiment (or Bhav, as known in Hindi).

Consciousness is effortless. Consciousness permeates every thought and visualization that occurs within one's mind. If the visualization is vibrant (indicating the presence of positive emotions), then it is this element that captivates the energy required for manifestation. Energy perpetually transforms into matter through unadulterated consciousness.

If one retrospectively examines their thoughts over the course of the day. It will be evident to you that the majority, amounting to 90 percent, of your thoughts are incongruous with your desired outcomes. Merely the portion representing 10 percent of your investment, specifically in the act of visualization, was observed, and the alignment of energies is contingent upon the level of engagement exhibited by the subconscious mind.

Therefore, if you are unable to envision the experience of possessing the automobile that you desire, it is unlikely that you will ever acquire it. The individual attempting to "manifest something" will never succeed in doing so, as it is primarily driven by ego. The ego cannot attain possession as it inherently contradicts the concept of possessing. The ego seizes, but does not accept. The ego expresses gratitude for acquiring, but it is not a passive act of receiving, rather an assertive act of appropriating from the universe. It is not operative in that manner. The ego may express appreciation with the intent of gaining something in return, yet fundamentally, such satisfaction represents a manifestation of avarice. Thus, what measures can be undertaken to address the hindrance of ego in our pursuit of manifesting our deepest aspirations? It is SIMPLE.

The book's effortless manifestation can be attributed to its composition with a noble intention: a deep-seated devotion to present it for God's perusal, rather than for personal gains. Therefore, despite possessing material aspirations and emotional needs for personal gratification, it is imperative to disregard these urges and direct one's endeavors towards the greater realm of the universe or the divine. This is Karma Yoga. It will facilitate the elevation of your vibrations to an extraordinary magnitude, bestowing upon you a divine perspective.

Cease fixating on desires and commence expressing gratitude for the blessings you currently possess. One effective and uncomplicated exercise entails meticulously documenting a list of 100 things for which you express gratitude. By recording a list of 100 items, an additional 100 items will likely manifest themselves to you. By composing a list of ten thousand elements to express your gratitude, another ten thousand elements shall manifest themselves unto you. One must simply cultivate genuine appreciation for those things.

These entities can encompass the vital oxygen that sustains respiration, the unobstructed nasal passages that facilitate smooth inhalation, the appreciation of possessing unimpaired physical faculties, or if faced with a disability, the gratitude that it does not surpass the current level of affliction. Expressing sincere gratitude for the privilege of having a place to call home and numerous other blessings.

Do you desire to cultivate a sense of gratitude for the very act of breathing in air?

Please occlude your nostrils using your fingers and attempt respiration with urgency for a duration of one minute. Now proceed to unveil them and observe the enhanced ease with which respiration can be achieved. Let us commence by expressing gratitude for 10 elements that are possessed by nearly all individuals.

Express your gratitude for the air you inhale.

Express gratitude for the nourishment you consume. Wild animals lack this form of comfort. To experience this sensation, it is advisable to undertake a

161

24-hour period of abstaining from food. You are likely to derive heightened enjoyment from the food, not on account of its enhanced taste, but rather due to a sense of gratitude and a profound longing to partake. Gratitude is only experienced upon the attainment of one's desires. It is not possible to express appreciation for something that is already in one's possession. This implies that if you inadvertently condition your mind to hold the belief that you do not desire what you are attempting to bring into reality. It will manifest. Alternatively, one can express appreciation for already possessing it, thereby materializing it within one's own sphere of existence. Express your appreciation for the fulfilment of your desires. Alternatively, express no appreciation due to the possession of the desired outcome (or relinquish that inclination entirely, thereby enabling its realization).

Show appreciation for the existence you hold within you.

Express your appreciation for the education that you have received thus far.

Express gratitude for the provision of hot water for bathing.

Express gratitude for the fact that you are currently wearing garments.

Express gratitude for possessing the knowledge required to generate anything.

the aspirations you have for your life.

Express appreciation for possessing the convenience and safeguard.

Express gratitude for the presence of companions and the ability to maintain connections with others amidst the challenges posed by the ongoing pandemic.

Express gratitude for your good health and existence.

Expressing deep appreciation and a sense of profound gratitude is the most profound sentiment one can experience upon receiving the materialization of one's desires. Each instance of manifestation is subsequently accompanied by expressions of appreciation and elevated energy frequencies. By expressing gratitude prior to the manifestation of your desires, you are in close proximity to achieving the very things you have yearned for. Every occurrence is a consequence of complete engagement in a mental imagery. Complete engagement refers to becoming fully immersed in your imagination to the extent that the external world becomes imperceptible. It does not truly vanish; rather, one's consciousness becomes deeply engrossed in a potential manifestation, refraining from diverting its attention elsewhere. Therefore, should one attempt to materialize something that is not genuinely appealing to the intellect, the resulting manifestation shall be feeble, yielding no remarkable outcomes.

So, what strategies can we employ to cultivate a robust inclination towards acquiring something? The outcome is contingent upon the location of your objectives. If your motivation for manifestation is primarily to seek validation and recognition from others, rather than solely visualizing the desired outcome, it is possible that your manifestation might not align with the specific object you envisioned, but rather manifest "receiving admiration and respect from others."

Why?

Due to your lack of desire for a luxurious automobile or an expansive residence. You just want to "feel important".

Know what you want.

May I effectively bring into existence that which I am envisioning? Indeed, it is imperative that you contemplate the emotions that would arise within you upon witnessing the physical manifestation of the visual content located beyond the confines of your living quarters in the present moment.

This particular exercise is highly beneficial for individuals of all backgrounds. Please ensure the door to your room is securely shut, and proceed to envision that all the elements you wish to visualize exist beyond the threshold. See how you feel. Remain indoors and engage in stillness, envisioning the state of readiness surrounding the area beyond the confines of this room. Envision the automobile that you have long desired, already situated outside your residence. Envision the funds you have already accumulated resting within the confines of the drawer. Please anticipate that it will remain in its designated location and in an organized manner upon opening the drawer. Gradually, as the passage of time unfolds, should you persist in the act of visualizing, the line between reality and the realm of your imagination shall gradually blur, leading to a state of being adrift in the latter.

Many athletes refer to this state of deep concentration as "The flow" state. This is the juncture at which co-creation takes place.

An additional crucial factor that necessitates our attention is the inherent nature of the mind. The inherent characteristic of the mind is such that regardless of the direction you steer it, it solely progresses in a forward trajectory, devoid of any regression. Hence, if I were to request that you cease contemplating apples, the mere suggestion of refraining from such thoughts may inadvertently evoke images of apples in your mind. You cannot resist thoughts. The thoughts will only gravitate towards their preferred destinations. Alternatively, it could be expressed as: "Put differently, thoughts lack autonomy over their own nature." The capacity for perception allows one to exercise discernment in observing specific types of thoughts.

Given the inherent characteristics of the intellect. Uncertainty and apprehension are intrinsic to human nature. Should you desire to experience anxiety, it shall indeed manifest itself within you. Should you choose to refrain from experiencing anxiety, you may find that your anxiety levels increase as a result. Thus, the resolution of this matter can solely be achieved through refraining from engaging with or indulging in manifestations of "anxiety". If you are indifferent to the presence or absence of anxiety. It will disappear. One cannot divert their attention towards contemplating apples while preoccupied with the deliberate effort of disregarding thoughts about mangoes. Although this may not be the finest demonstration, it effectively conveys the intended message. The mind lacks agency as it is bound by the inherent nature of all things. EVERYTHING EXPANDS. When one directs their awareness towards something, it undergoes a process of expansion. If one contemplates a desired object, said object shall grow in one's mind and shall eventually manifest itself when one is sufficiently prepared. The principle of the law of attraction can be succinctly summarized as such. The complications arise due to the influence of one's ego.

Astonishing Quality of Awareness?!

Have you ever observed that when you engage in the practice of meditation or focus your attention on a specific region of your body, such as the area between your eyebrows, muscular contractions or involuntary movements occur in that particular area? This phenomenon occurs due to the concentration of one's awareness, which subsequently leads to the accumulation of energy in the respective location. Awareness has the ability to draw energy towards itself. If one were to employ their consciousness in a forceful manner at a specific region of their body, that region would inevitably undergo a perceptible advancement in physical aging.

Similarly, thoughts and emotions experience growth when they are nourished by your conscious attention. Should you assume the state of being the adjacent plant, you would find that it accelerates its growth due to the infusion of energy facilitated by your heightened consciousness. Energy can solely manifest in physical shape via cognition, or more precisely, consciousness. Awareness and consciousness are commonly regarded as synonymous, and as such, I have employed them interchangeably.

The self (or one's sense of individuality) will inquire, fret, and oppose.

What if I fail? Does it really happen? What if I am unable to contemplate this matter? Why does my capacity for imagination appear to be lacking? The origin of these resistances lies within the cognitive realm, and their eradication can solely be accomplished through cognitive means.

How to erase them?

Cease contemplating the issues and instead divert your thoughts towards your desired outcomes. It can be ascertained that you are aware that a mere shift in thought has the potential to induce a negative emotional state. You are on the cusp of obtaining all that you have ever desired, requiring only a single thought to bridge the gap. An additional crucial aspect that warrants discussion pertains to the outcomes. If the desired outcomes are not observed, the ego swiftly comprehends this discrepancy and begins to question the circumstances, timing, and rationale behind it. The concept of ego exhibits a propensity for cunning and deceptive behavior. It displays a remarkable degree of naivety and a desire to abstain from acquiring anything solely out of fear of potential consequences involved in acquiring and not utilizing them. In terms of self-pride, manifestation pertains essentially to promptly acquiring all desired things from the universe. Ego can never receive, because if it ever does, it won't be able to claim absolute authority over it. This indicates that cultivating emotions of surrender and gratitude is pivotal for manifesting one's desires. The ego is inherently deprived, lacking the capacity to possess but rather desires. There exists only a singular distinction between harboring a desire and possessing a want. It is greed.

www.ingramcontent.com/pod-product-compliance
Lightning Source LLC
Chambersburg PA
CBHW071127050326
40690CB00008B/1361